Jupiter, Neptune
and Other
Outer Planets

Chris Oxlade

First published in Great Britain in 2007
by Wayland, an imprint of Hachette Children's Books

This paperback edition published in 2009
by Wayland, an imprint of Hachette Children's Books

Wayland
338 Euston Road, London NW1 3BH

Editor: Nicola Edwards
Designer: Tim Mayer
Consultant: Ian Graham

British Library Cataloguing in Publication Data
Oxlade, Chris
    Jupiter, Neptune and other outer planets. -
    (Earth and space)
    1. Outer planets - Juvenile literature
    I. Title
    523.4

ISBN : 9780750249973

Wayland is a division of Hachette Children's Books,
an Hachette UK Company.
www.hachettelivre.co.uk

Cover photograph: Jupiter, the largest planet in the
Solar System, with one of its 63 moons.

Photo credits: Bettmann/Corbis:44; Chris Butler/SPL:
37; John Chumack/SPL: 33; Chris Cooke/SPL: 7; Corbis:
front cover; ESA; 40; Mark Garlick/SPL: 11, 19, 25, 29,
35; David A. Hardy/SPL: 13b, 43; JPL/Cal
Tech/NASA/Corbis: 8; JPL/NASA: 21; Lunar &
Planetary Institute: 6; NASA: 1, 5, 10, 13t, 14t, 14b,
15, 16, 17b, 18, 20, 23, 24, 27t, 27b, 28, 31, 39, 41,
45; NASA/ESA/STSCI/A Stern,SWRI/SPL: 34;
NASA/JHUAPL/SWRI/SPL: 42; NASA/SPL: 22, 23t, 30,
36; Detlev van Ravenswaay/SPL: 32; Roger
Ressmeyer/Corbis: 9, 38; Roger
Ressmeyer/NASA/Corbis: 12, 17t; Dennis Scott/Corbis:
26.

The website addresses (URLs) included in this book
were valid at the time of going to press. However,
because of the nature of the Internet, it is possible
that some addresses may have changed, or sites may
have changed or closed down since publication.
While the author and publisher regret any
inconvenience this may cause the readers, no
responsibility for any such changes can be accepted
by either the author or the publisher.

Contents

The Outer Planets

Our Earth is 150 million kilometres from the Sun. Here, the Sun lights our planet and we can feel its warmth. In the far reaches of the Solar System are four planets that are very different from the Earth. They are cold worlds, hardly warmed at all by the Sun.

The Solar System

In the Solar System, the Sun is surrounded by a family of eight planets. A planet is a large object that orbits the Sun. Some of the planets are smaller than Earth, and some are larger. Each planet has its own unique features, but we can divide them into two main groups. One group is made up of the four planets nearest the Sun, which are Mercury, Venus, Earth and Mars. These planets have rocky surfaces. They are known as the inner planets, or the rocky, or terrestrial planets.

The other group is made up of the other four planets furthest from the Sun, namely Jupiter, Saturn, Uranus and Neptune. These planets are much bigger than the inner planets, and are made up of gas. They are known as the outer planets, the giant planets, or the gas giants.

The Solar System does not stop at Neptune. There are thousands of small, icy bodies beyond. Pluto was classed as a planet until 2006. Then experts at the International Astronomical Union downgraded it to a 'dwarf planet' because it is just one of these icy objects.

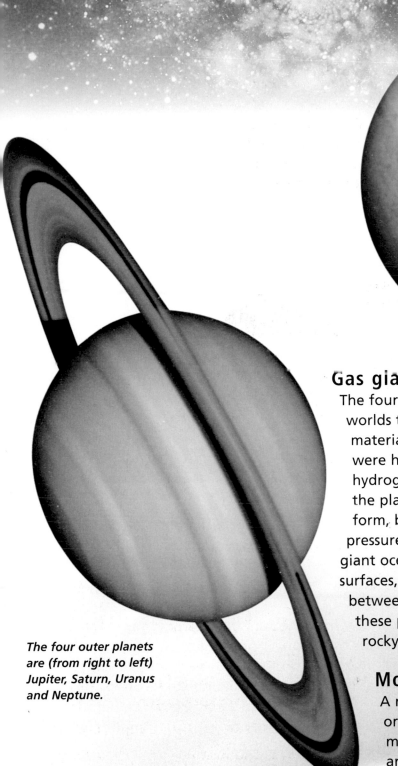

Gas giants

The four gas giants are very different worlds to the Earth. They are made of materials that would be gases if they were here on the Earth, such as hydrogen and helium. On the outside of the planets, the materials are in gas form, but deeper inside the planet, pressure turns them into liquids, forming giant oceans. The planets don't have surfaces, as there is no distinct boundary between the gas and liquid. Deep inside, these planets probably have a small, rocky core.

The four outer planets are (from right to left) Jupiter, Saturn, Uranus and Neptune.

Moons and rings

A moon is a large, rocky body that orbits a planet. The gas giants have many moons each, some of which are larger than the planet Mercury. Jupiter has more than sixty moons. All the gas giants also have rings around them, made up of chunks of rock and ice. Saturn's ring system is the most spectacular.

Moving Through Space

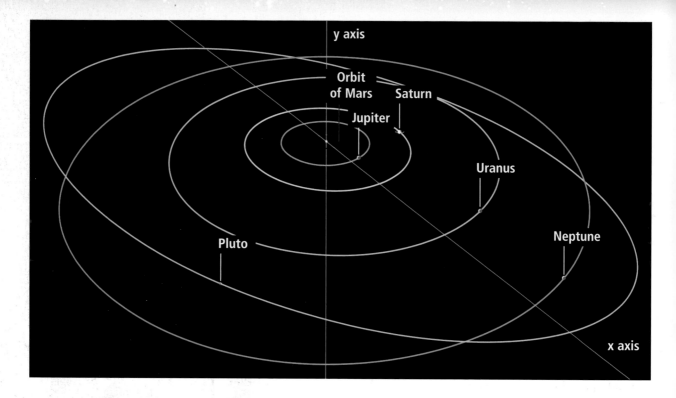

y axis

Orbit of Mars

Saturn

Jupiter

Uranus

Pluto

Neptune

x axis

The orbits of the four outer planets (Mars is shown as the last of the inner planets), and of Pluto, which sometimes moves inside the orbit of Neptune. The Sun is at the centre of the orbits.

All the planets travel in the same direction around the Sun in paths called orbits. The orbits of the gas giants are shaped like slightly squashed circles. The planets also spin as they move through space.

How the planets orbit
The further a planet is from the Sun, the slower it moves along its orbit, and the longer its orbit is. For example, Uranus orbits further from the Sun than Jupiter. It orbits at half the speed of Jupiter, and takes seven times as long as Jupiter to complete its orbit. The Sun is not right in the centre of the planets' squashed orbits, but slightly to one side. This means that a planet moves closer to and further from the Sun as it moves along its orbit.

How the planets spin
The outer planets spin as they move along their orbits. Each one spins around an imaginary line called its axis. Its poles are where its axis comes out through the surface.

The Sun lights up the side of a planet nearest to it, and as the planet spins, parts of the planet move in and out of the sunlight, giving daytime and night-time. The moons also spin as they orbit their planets.

We see the outer planets because sunlight bounces off them. Jupiter and Saturn look like very bright stars in the night sky. The other outer planets can only be seen with a telescope.

Days and years

The movements of the planets give them days and years. A day is the time between one sunrise and the next at any given place on the planet. The faster a planet spins, the shorter its day. Despite their enormous size, the gas giants have days that are shorter than an Earth day. A year is the time it takes for a planet to complete an orbit of the Sun. Years on the outer planets last for tens or hundreds of Earth years.

Gravity

The force of gravity keeps the planets in orbit around the Sun. Gravity attracts the planets to the Sun. It acts like a string, stopping the planets from flying off into space, and holding them in their orbits. Gravity also attracts the moons to their planets, keeping them in orbit.

In the night sky, Saturn looks like a very bright star as sunlight reflects from it.

How the Planets Formed

Astronomers think that all the planets in our Solar System were formed about 4,600 million years ago, after the Sun was formed. The planets, including the gas giants, all came from a wispy cloud of gas and dust.

Space Facts

Atoms in space

- The space between the planets is not completely empty. There are a few atoms in every cubic centimetre. The air you breathe contains about 25 billion billion atoms per cubic centimetre.

- The atoms in space take billions of years to drift together and form the nebulae that stars and planets are born from.

The Solar System began to form nearly 5 billion years ago from part of a vast cloud of gas and dust, known as a nebula. Very, very slowly, over millions of years, gravity pulled the particles of gas and dust together into clumps. As the clumps formed, they also began to spin. Eventually, gravity pulled the clumps of gas and dust into enormous, super-dense balls. Intense heat and pressure in the centre of the balls started nuclear reactions. Energy from these reactions left the balls as heat, light and radiation. One of the glowing balls was our Sun.

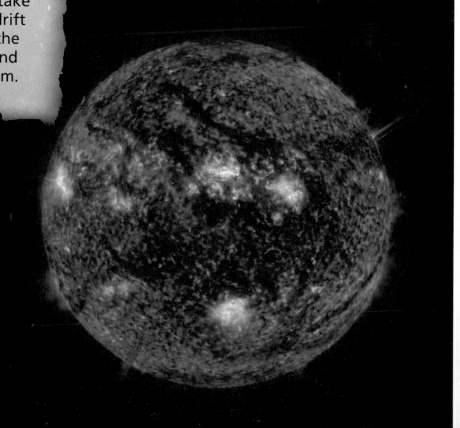

The Sun is by far the largest body in the Solar System. It is nearly a thousand times more massive than Jupiter, the largest planet.

A spinning disc

Astronomers think the planets formed from a spinning disc of rocky particles, dust and gas that was left over after the formation of the Sun. As the Sun began to shine more brightly, its heat and radiation turned any icy material close to it into gas, and pushed it away, towards the outer edge of the disc. This gaseous material included water vapour, hydrogen and helium.

It took millions of years for all the material that makes up the giant planet Jupiter to come together.

Planetesimals

Meanwhile, the particles of rock and dust continued to move around the Sun. When two particles collided, they sometimes stuck together, forming larger particles. Very slowly, gravity pulled these larger particles together until large boulders, called planetesimals formed. Eventually gravity pulled the planetesimals together, too, forming huge rocky lumps.

In the inner Solar System, these lumps formed the inner, rocky planets. In the outer Solar System, they formed the rocky cores of the outer planets. These cores attracted the gases in the outer Solar System, which formed the planets' thick outer layers.

The material left over from the disc around the Sun also formed the moons around the planets, and all the other bodies in the Solar System. These include the asteroids that orbit the Sun between Mars and Jupiter, and thousands of icy bodies that orbit beyond Neptune.

Jupiter

Jupiter is the fifth planet from the Sun and the first of the outer planets. It is the largest planet in the Solar System. From Earth, Jupiter looks like a very bright star. Through a telescope, you can see that Jupiter is covered with swirling bands of brown and yellow clouds, and violent storms.

Orbit and spin

Jupiter orbits more than three times further away from the Sun than Mars, the outermost of the inner planets. Jupiter takes nearly twelve Earth years to complete an orbit, but it completes a spin on its axis in just 9 hours and 55 minutes. It spins more quickly at its equator than at its poles. This can happen because the upper layers of Jupiter are not solid, but made of liquid and gas. Jupiter's high-speed spin makes its middle bulge outwards, so it is slightly flattened. It measures 133,708 km between the poles, but 142,984 km across at the equator.

Jupiter's structure

Jupiter is a really huge planet. It contains twice as much matter as all the other planets and moons in the Solar System put together. It is more than eleven times wider than the Earth, and 1,321 Earths could fit inside it.

Jupiter's spectacular bands of cloud, seen by the Hubble Space Telescope.

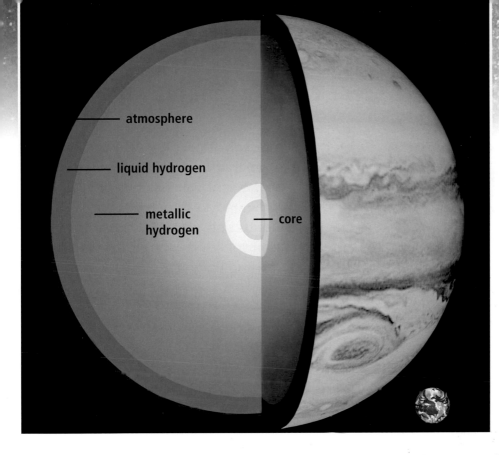

atmosphere

liquid hydrogen

metallic
hydrogen

core

This is what the inside of Jupiter may look like. It is made up mostly of hydrogen.

Astronomers don't actually know what the inside of Jupiter is like, but they know how large and how heavy the planet is, and what the atmosphere is made from. This allows them to have a good guess at what's inside. They think that Jupiter has a core made up mostly of iron, which is quite small compared to the overall size of the planet. The pressure in the core is immense, and the temperature is about 20,000°C.

Around the core is a layer of metallic hydrogen. The hydrogen is metallic because of the huge pressure inside the planet. The hydrogen acts like a liquid metal, such as mercury, rather than a normal liquid. This allows it to conduct electricity, and its movement creates Jupiter's powerful magnetic field. On top of this layer is a layer of liquid hydrogen. Surrounding the liquid layer is an atmosphere. This is also made mostly of hydrogen, with some helium, but this time in gas form.

SPACE DATA

Jupiter

Diameter (equator):	142,984 km
Average distance from Sun:	778,330,000 km
Time to complete one orbit:	11 Earth years 10 months
Time to complete one spin:	9 Earth hours 55 minutes
Gravity at surface:	2.64 x Earth gravity
Surface temperature:	-150°C
Number of moons:	63

Jupiter: the Atmosphere

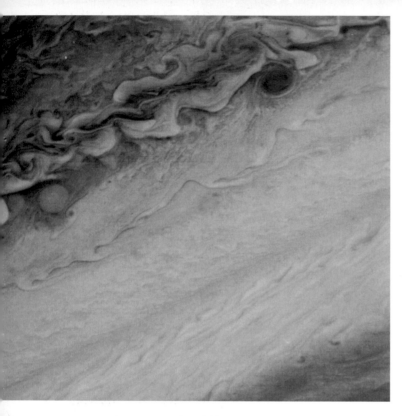

A close-up of Jupiter's swirling cloud bands.

Jupiter's atmosphere is very shallow compared to the size of the planet – just as an apple's skin is thin compared to the rest of the fruit. Clouds and powerful currents in the atmosphere create Jupiter's dramatic, swirling bands of colour.

Gases and clouds

Jupiter's atmosphere is made up mainly of hydrogen and helium. In the upper atmosphere there are three layers of clouds. The clouds in each layer are made up of billions of tiny crystals, just as clouds on Earth are made up of droplets of water or crystals of water ice.

Clouds in the top layer of Jupiter's atmosphere are made of crystals of ammonia, called ammonia ice. The clouds in the second layer are made up of a chemical called ammonium hydrosulphide. The lower layer's clouds are made of water ice.

The different-coloured bands of cloud move in opposite directions around the planet. They move at incredibly high speeds. They are blown along by high-level winds of 500 kilometres per hour or more, similar to the jet streams in Earth's upper atmosphere.

How do we know?
Exploring Jupiter

Astronomers didn't really know that the Great Red Spot was a storm system (see page 13), until the probes *Pioneer 10* and *Pioneer 11* visited Jupiter in the mid 1970s. By the end of that decade the *Voyager* probes had sent back detailed photographs of the cloud bands and storms. In 1995, the *Galileo* spacecraft dropped a mini-probe into Jupiter's atmosphere. It sent back data about the chemicals in the atmosphere, and the winds and temperatures.

The clouds swirl tightly along the edges of the bands, where the winds are blowing in opposite directions. The light bands are called zones, and are made up of high-level ammonia clouds. The darker, red-brown bands are called belts. Scientists are not sure what causes their colour.

Jupiter's Great Red Spot is the Solar System's biggest storm system.

Swirling storms

As well as moving bands of cloud, there are giant storms in Jupiter's atmosphere. These pull the clouds into swirling patterns. The storms grow and fade. There is one enormous storm known as the Great Red Spot. It is an oval-shaped storm of red clouds, about 26,000 kilometres across, sandwiched between two bands of cloud. The Great Red Spot has been raging for at least three hundred years, although it sometimes fades. There are also enormous thunderstorms on Jupiter. Jupiter is too far from the Sun for the Sun's heat to drive the storms. The heat that causes them comes from inside the planet.

Technicians working on the Galileo probe before its launch.

Jupiter: the Moons and Ring

Jupiter has more moons that any other planet. So far, astronomers have discovered 63 moons orbiting the planet. Some are giant moons as large as planets, and some just a few kilometres across.

Jupiter's moon Callisto has a dark, cratered surface.

Large and small

Jupiter has four moons that are many times larger than the other moons. In order from Jupiter, they are Io, Europa, Ganymede and Callisto. These moons, visible from Earth through binoculars, were discovered in 1610 by the Italian astronomer Galileo, which is why they are known as the Galilean moons. The spins of all the Galilean moons are locked to Jupiter. The moons complete one spin each time they complete one orbit of Jupiter, so the same side of each moon faces Jupiter all the time, just as same side of the Moon faces the Earth all the time. The rest of Jupiter's moons are tiny compared to the Galilean moons. The largest, called Amalthea, is just 270 kilometres across. Jupiter's small moons were discovered by the *Voyager* probes and the *Galileo* probe, and from Earth through powerful telescopes.

The four Galilean moons orbiting above Jupiter are (from bottom right) Callisto, Ganymede, Europa and Io.

The Galilean moons have some very interesting features. Io is covered with active volcanoes. Europa is covered with a cracked, icy surface. Ganymede is the largest moon in the Solar System. It is even larger than Mercury, the smallest of the inner, rocky planets. You can find out more about Io, Europa and Ganymede on page 16.

Ganymede's surface is covered with ridges and craters.

How the moons orbit

Jupiter's moons orbit the planet in different zones. There are groups of moons in close, medium and far zones. Between these zones are huge, moon-free gaps. A group of small moons orbit less than 150,000 kilometres out. The Galilean moons are next. They orbit between 420,000 kilometres and 1.9 million kilometres out. There is another group of moons between 11 and 12 million kilometres. Then there is a gap until about 20 million kilometres, where dozens of tiny moons orbit. All the moons here orbit in the opposite direction to the other moons. They are probably asteroids captured by Jupiter's gravity.

Jupiter's rings

Jupiter has a single main ring (a band of material around the planet). Jupiter's main ring is about 7,000 kilometres across but very, very thin. It is made from tiny dust particles, and is too faint to see from Earth. There are also extremely faint rings inside and outside the main ring, called the halo and gossamer rings.

SPACE DATA

Jupiter's Moons

Total number
of moons: 63

Largest moon: Ganymede (diameter
                     5,260 km)

Closest moon
to Jupiter: Metis (57,000 km
                     from surface)

Furthest moon
from Jupiter: S/2003 J2 (28,500,000
                     km from surface)

Jupiter: Galilean Moons

Io, Europa, Ganymede and Callisto are the four Galilean moons of Jupiter. Io, Europa and Ganymede have very interesting features, whereas Callisto, the third largest moon in the Solar System, is a dead, cratered world.

Io

Io is similar in size to Earth's Moon. It is one of the most volcanically active bodies in the Solar System. More than a hundred active volcanoes spew out lava and fountains of liquid sulphur. The sulphur creates red, orange and yellow patterns on the surface. One of Io's volcanoes, called Loki, is more powerful than all the Earth's active volcanoes combined.

Jupiter's moon Europa has a smooth, cracked, icy surface.

Io's active volcanoes mean that there must be plenty of heat inside the moon. Scientists think that the gravity of Jupiter and Europa keeps stretching and squashing Io, making the inside heat up. This effect is called tidal heating.

Europa

Europa is the smallest of the Galilean moons. Its surface looks very similar to a frozen sea on Earth, with the icy crust broken into giant pieces. Scientists think that there may be a huge ocean of water under this icy surface. The cracks could be caused by the ice breaking, allowing water to seep out and freeze. The heat to stop the ocean freezing solid could be generated by tidal heating (see above). Scientists think that there may be a chance of finding life in Europa's ocean.

Ganymede

Ganymede is the largest moon in the Solar System. Like Europa it has an icy crust. But unlike Europa, there are many craters littering the surface. These were caused by a bombardment of debris in the moon's early life. There are also ridges and grooves on the surface, which may have been caused by heat from inside the moon. There may be liquid water under the surface.

In this photograph of Io, a plume rises from a volcano top left.

How do we know?

Visiting Jupiter's moons

Io's volcanoes were discovered in 1979 by the *Voyager* probes. *Voyager 2* photographed a giant fountain of sulphur erupting from the surface. Further investigations of the Galilean moons were made by the *Galileo* craft, which arrived at Jupiter in 1995. It photographed more eruptions from Io, and its sensors detected signs of liquid water under Europa's icy surface. *Galileo* also discovered some new moons.

Saturn

One of the first close-up images of Saturn, taken by the *Pioneer 11* probe in 1979.

Saturn is the sixth planet from the Sun. It is a little smaller than Jupiter, but easily the second largest planet in the Solar System. Its system of rings, clearly visible from Earth through a telescope, makes it the most beautiful and spectacular planet of all.

Orbit and spin

Saturn is nearly 1,500 million kilometres from the Sun. That's about twice as far from the Sun as Jupiter. It takes nearly 30 Earth years to complete one orbit. Saturn spins very quickly on its axis. It completes a spin in just 10 hours and 40 minutes. This means that the equator of Saturn moves at an incredible 36,000 kilometres per hour. This makes the equator bulge outwards, making the planet slightly squashed. Saturn measures 108,728 kilometres between the poles, but 120,536 km across at the equator.

Saturn's structure

Saturn is almost ten times wider than the Earth, and its mass is ninety-five times greater than the Earth. But its density is much less than the Earth because Saturn is made mostly of hydrogen, which is the lightest chemical there is. In fact, if you could find an ocean large enough, Saturn would float in it. We don't know what the inside of Saturn looks like, but astronomers can make assumptions from knowing its size, mass, and what its atmosphere is made of.

They think that Saturn has a core made up mostly of iron, which is larger than the Earth. Around the core is a layer of metallic hydrogen. The immense pressure inside the planet makes the hydrogen act like liquid metal, such as mercury (see page 11). On top of this layer is a layer of liquid hydrogen. Surrounding the liquid layer is an atmosphere, again made mostly of hydrogen, but this time in gas form, with a little helium.

Saturn's atmosphere

Saturn's atmosphere of hydrogen is about 400 kilometres thick. Bands of clouds move around the planet in opposite directions, blown by winds of up to 1,800 kilometres per hour. Occasionally, swirling storms form. They are seen as white spots as their clouds are made up of ammonia ice. The temperature at the top of the atmosphere is −180°C.

This is what Saturn's internal structure is thought to be like.

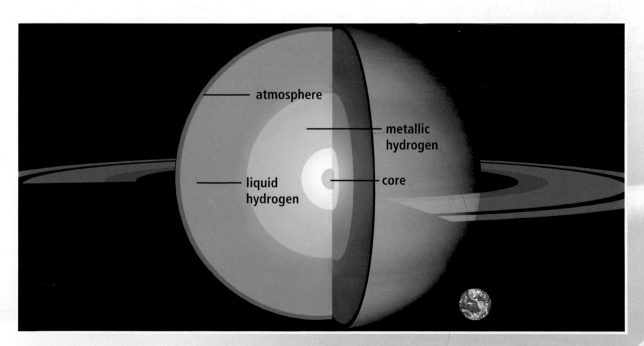

atmosphere

metallic hydrogen

liquid hydrogen

core

Saturn: the Rings

A close-up of Saturn's C ring (blue) and B ring (orange). The colours have been added to the image.

Saturn's spectacular rings are made of billions of chunks of ice that orbit the planet. The ice reflects sunlight well, making the rings very bright. From the inner edge to the outer edge, the rings cover more than 400,000 kilometres, which is further than the distance from the Earth to its Moon.

Rings and ringlets

Saturn has seven main rings. Each ring has its own density and mixture of large and small particles, which is why the rings look slightly different to each other. The rings are very thin compared to their width. For example, the second ring from the planet (the C ring – see below) is 17,300 kilometres wide, but just 5 metres deep. Some of the rings are actually made up of hundreds of thousands or millions of thin rings, known as ringlets. The third ring out from Saturn (the B ring) has many dark streaks running across it, like the spokes of a wheel. These may be made of small dust particles.

Ring names

Astronomers have given the rings letters to identify them. The closest ring to Jupiter is called the D ring. Its inner edge is just 6,400 kilometres from the planet. Then come the C, B and A rings, which are the brightest rings. Next is a very thin ring, the F ring, followed by the G ring. Finally comes the giant E ring, which is 302,000 kilometres across. The E ring is made of very fine particles, which makes it very faint.

Rings gaps

There are several gaps between Saturn's rings. Between the A ring and B ring is a 4,590-kilometre gap called the Cassini Division. There is also a gap in the A ring, known as the Encke Division, where a moon called Atlas orbits.

Origin of the rings

Astronomers think that the material that makes up Saturn's rings came from moons, comets or asteroids that were broken up by Jupiter's gravity. When an object such as an asteroid moves into orbit very close to a planet, the planet's gravity slowly pulls it apart. The pieces around Saturn would then have orbited at different speeds, spreading out to form the rings.

The colours in this image represent the sizes of particles in each ring.

Saturn: the Moons

A false-colour image of Saturn's moon Titan, taken by the Cassini probe.

So far, astronomers have discovered 56 moons orbiting Saturn. They range in size from Titan, which is almost half as wide as the Earth, to rocky lumps just a few kilometres across. Most moons are made of ice. Titan is one the most intriguing moons in the Solar System.

Shepherd moons

Many of the moons orbit inside Saturn's rings, or in the gaps in the rings. The gravity of four of these inner moons, Pan, Atlas, Prometheus and Pandora, helps to shape the rings by pulling on their particles. These moons are known as shepherd moons because they control the rings like shepherds control sheep. Other moons sweep along the gaps, keeping them clear.

Titan

Titan is the second largest moon in the Solar System (Jupiter's moon Ganymede is the largest), and the only moon in the Solar System with a dense atmosphere. Haze and clouds in the atmosphere make the surface invisible from space. Titan is far too cold for liquid water to exist. But it does rain here. The rain is made from drops of methane. Complex chemicals also form in the atmosphere and fall to the surface.

Titan's surface has solid land with mountains and valleys, and seas. The valleys were not cut by water, but by liquid methane, which also fills the seas. The mountains are made from water ice. There is a large feature like a continent, which has been named Xanadu.

Titan is a strange place, but scientists believe the Earth could have been similar in its early life. So studying Titan could tell us something about the Earth's early life, and possibly even how life began here.

More moon features

The moon Enceladus has volcanoes that spew out water that freezes to form ice. Particles from these volcanoes may form part of Saturn's E ring. Both Mimas and Tethys have giant impact craters. The collisions may have temporarily broken up the moons. Some moons share orbits. For example, Tethys, Calypso and Telesto all orbit on the same path.

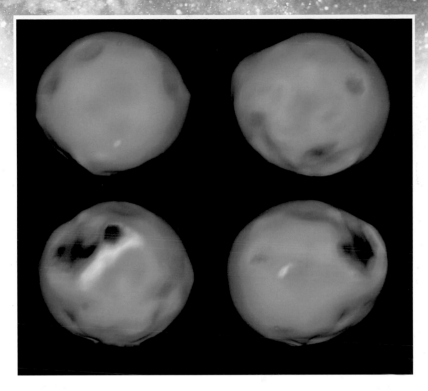

A computer model of Saturn's moon Phoebe, using data from the Cassini *probe.*

The Cassini-Huygens *probe ready to be launched to Saturn.*

How do we know?

The *Cassini-Huygens* probe

The *Cassini-Huygens* probe has made many new discoveries about Titan. The probe was made up of *Cassini*, designed to orbit Saturn, and *Huygens*, a smaller craft designed to land on Titan. The probe was launched in 1997, and entered orbit around Saturn in 2004. *Huygens* descended to Titan in early 2005. It dropped slowly through Titan's atmosphere, taking two-and-a-half hours to reach the surface. It sent back photographs of Titan, and data about the atmosphere.

Uranus

Uranus is the seventh planet from the Sun. It is another of the gas giants. It is four times as wide as Earth, midway in size between the large gas giants (Jupiter and Saturn) and the rocky planets. Unlike Jupiter and Saturn, Uranus is very hard to see from Earth.

Orbit and spin

Uranus is an extremely long way from the Sun. It orbits twice as far out as it neighbour, Saturn. It takes just under 84 Earth years to complete an orbit. Some of the other planets, including Earth, are tipped over slightly, but Uranus is tipped over completely. This means that Uranus orbits the Sun on its side. Sometimes during its orbit, its axis points almost at the Sun.

This Voyager 2 *image shows Uranus's hazy atmosphere.*

Uranus's side-on spin produces seasons on the planet. When its north pole is pointing towards the Sun, the planet's northern hemisphere has summer, and when the north pole is pointing away from the Sun, it has winter. Because Uranus is so tilted, the seasons are extreme. Each pole receives continuous sunlight for 42 years, followed by continuous darkness for 42 years. Even so, the difference between summer and winter is very small. Not much of the Sun's heat reaches Uranus. The summer Sun only warms the poles by about 2°C. On average, the temperature of the cloud tops is a freezing –215°C.

SPACE DATA

Uranus

Diameter (equator):	51,118 km
Average distance from Sun:	2,872,500,000 km
Time to complete one orbit:	83 Earth years 10 months
Time to complete one spin:	17 Earth hours 12 minutes
Gravity at surface:	0.89 x Earth gravity
Surface temperature:	-215°C
Number of moons:	27

Uranus's structure

Uranus has a deep atmosphere made up mostly of hydrogen, mixed with helium and a small amount of methane. At the bottom of the atmosphere is a deep layer of liquid hydrogen, and then a layer made up of water, ammonia and methane. In the centre of Uranus is a rocky core.

Atmosphere

Uranus has an atmosphere much deeper than that of Jupiter or Saturn, but much less interesting to look at. The whole planet is hazy blue-green because of crystals of methane ice in the upper atmosphere. There are just a few wispy white clouds. Their movement shows that winds of 300 km/h can blow through the atmosphere.

This is what astronomers think the internal structure of the planet Uranus is like.

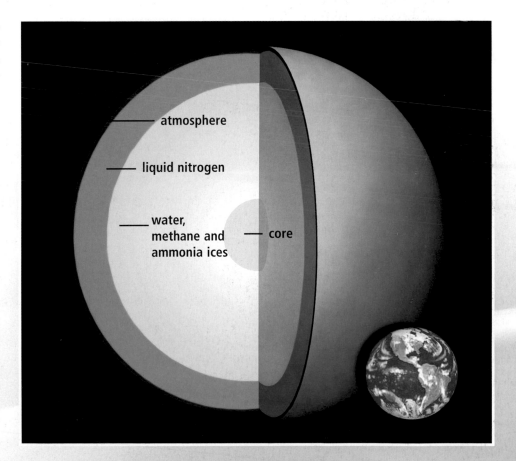

atmosphere

liquid nitrogen

water, methane and ammonia ices

core

Uranus: the Rings and Moons

Like Jupiter and Saturn, Uranus has many moons and a set of rings. So far, 27 moons have been discovered, ranging in size from more than a thousand kilometres across to just a few kilometres across.

An artist's impression of Uranus and its faint ring system.

Dark rings

Uranus has a set of rings. They are like Saturn's rings, but not as extensive, and they are also made from dark, rocky material, rather than ice. Each narrow ring is made up of billions of boulders. There are twelve rings altogether, ten between 42,000 and 51,000 kilometres from the centre of the planet, and two more 100,000 kilometres out. Because the rings are dark, and because they are so far from Earth, they can't be seen with telescopes. They were only discovered in 1977, when Uranus moved in front of a star. Then astronomers were able to see the light from the star fade and brighten as the rings moved across it.

Moons

Uranus has five large moons (known as the major moons), called Miranda, Ariel, Umbriel, Titania and Oberon. Titania is the largest moon, at 1,578 km across. Miranda is the smallest, at 470 km across, but it is also the most interesting. The rest of the moons are very much smaller. The two closest moons to the planet, Cordelia and Ophelia, keep some of the rings in shape with their gravity, and are known as shepherd moons (see page 22). Cordelia orbits inside the rings. There are more small moons millions of kilometres from Uranus, which mostly orbit in the opposite direction to the large moons.

Voyager 2 *waiting for launch in 1977. The probe is inside the top section of the rocket.*

How do we know?

Voyager 2 visits Uranus

The probe *Voyager 2* is the only space probe to have visited Uranus. It arrived in 1986, eight and a half years after leaving Earth. It flew very close to Uranus, just 80,000 kilometres away from the cloud tops. *Voyager 2* discovered ten new moons, two new rings, and Uranus's magnetic field. It also gave astronomers their first close-up views of the remarkable moons.

Miranda

Uranus's moon Miranda has one of the strangest surfaces of any body in the Solar System. Some areas are covered with cliffs and mountains, others with cracks or canyons, and other areas are smooth, or cratered. Astronomers think that Miranda may have been smashed apart by a giant collision, and then pulled back together again, ending up like a muddled jigsaw.

The complex surface of Miranda, photographed by Voyager 2.

27

Neptune

Neptune

Diameter (equator):	49,528 km
Average distance from Sun:	4,495,100,000 km
Time to complete one orbit:	164 Earth years 10 months
Time to complete one spin:	16 Earth hours 7 minutes
Gravity at surface:	1.12 x Earth gravity
Surface temperature:	-214°C
Number of moons:	13

Neptune is the eighth planet from the Sun, and the last of the gas giants. Neptune is very similar to Uranus. It is almost the same size, and is made of the same material. However, Neptune has a much more active atmosphere than Uranus.

Orbit and spin

In an average human lifetime, Neptune does not even manage half an orbit! Neptune orbits 4,500 million kilometres from the Sun, half as far again as Uranus. It takes almost 165 Earth years to complete an orbit. Like the other gas giants, its spins fast, completing a spin in just over sixteen hours.

Neptune's structure

Neptune has an atmosphere made up mostly of hydrogen, mixed with helium and a small amount of methane. At the bottom of the atmosphere is a deep layer of liquid hydrogen, and then a layer made up of water, ammonia and methane. In the centre of Neptune is a molten rocky core.

Neptune has faint bands of blue clouds, with light and dark patches.

Neptune's atmosphere

Neptune's blue colour comes from clouds of methane ice. There are dark patches and streaks of white in the blue background. Winds blow around Neptune in both directions. They blow at speeds of up to 2,200 km/h, making Neptune the windiest planet in the Solar System. The dark patches are storm systems. One of these, which has now disappeared, was as wide as the Earth, and known as the Great Dark Spot. Another is oval-shaped, with a white centre, and known as the Great Dark Spot 2 or the Wizard's Eye. Neptune's atmosphere is extremely cold. The temperature at the cloud tops is -214°C.

How do we know?
Discovering Neptune

Neptune was discovered by mathematics rather than by looking through a telescope. Studies of Uranus showed that there are slight wobbles in its orbit. These could only be caused by the gravity of another object. So astronomers thought there must be another planet beyond Uranus that nobody knew about. Two mathematicians used the laws of motion to work out exactly where the unknown planet would be. German astronomer Johann Galle found Neptune in 1846, looking exactly where mathematicians had predicted.

Astronomers think that the internal structure of Neptune is like this.

atmosphere

liquid hydrogen

water, ammonia and methane ices

core

Neptune: its Rings and Moons

Like the other gas giants, Neptune has a set of rings, and many moons. So far, astronomers have discovered six rings and thirteen moons. The moon Triton is about three-quarters the size of the Earth's Moon.

An image of Neptune's two main rings, taken by the Voyager 2 *probe.*

Clumpy rings

Neptune has two wide rings and four narrow rings. The widest, called Lassell, is about 4,000 kilometres across. All the rings are made of dark material, and are very dim, so they are difficult to see. They are made up of very small particles.

The outermost ring, called Adams, is a peculiar ring. Its particles are clumped together in several places. This makes the ring look darker in some parts than others. From a distance, it looks as though the Adams ring is made up of arcs (parts of a circle) with gaps in between. The clumps are probably caused by the gravity of a moon called Galatea, which orbits very close to the Adams ring.

Moons

Triton is Neptune's major moon, with a radius of 1,353 kilometres. It is also the only spherical moon. The other moons are much smaller, and irregular in shape, like giant potatoes. Triton and Nereid are the only moons of Neptune that can be seen from Earth through telescopes.

Triton's icy surface reflects most of the dim sunlight that shines on it.

How do we know?
Voyager 2 at Neptune

Much of our knowledge of Neptune comes from the *Voyager 2* probe, which is the only probe to have visited Neptune. It took *Voyager 2* twelve years to reach Neptune. On arrival, it discovered six new moons and confirmed that there was a system of rings.

Neptune's moons orbit in groups. Several small moons orbit very close to the planet, and some orbit inside the rings. Then comes a gap until Triton. Nereid orbits more than ten times further out. More small moons orbit between about 15 million and about 47 million kilometres out.

Triton

The surface of Triton is covered with cracks. These were probably formed when the surface melted and then froze again. Triton's south pole is covered with methane ice, which has a slightly pink colour made by other chemicals mixed with the methane. In some places the ice is covered with dark streaks. These are caused by dust that is thrown into the atmosphere by volcanoes, is carried along by the wind, and then falls to the surface. Triton is the coldest object in the Solar System, with a surface temperature of -236°C. Triton also orbits in the opposite direction to most of Neptune's other moons.

Beyond Neptune

The Solar System does not stop at Neptune. There are millions of objects further out in space. All these objects are icy bodies. They are made of material left over after the formation of the Sun and the planets. Together, they are known as trans-Neptunian objects.

The Kuiper Belt

Beyond the orbit of Neptune there is a region of space where there are many icy, planet-like objects, known as the Kuiper Belt. The distances of these objects from the Sun are so huge that they are measured in astronomical units (au). One astronomical unit is equal to the distance between the Sun and Earth, which is 150 million kilometres. The Kuiper Belt stretches from about 30 au to about 50 au from the Sun.

An artist's impression of icy objects in the Kuiper Belt, beyond Neptune.

Space Facts

Trans-Neptunian objects

- Sedna has a very stretched orbit, which will take it as far as 900 au from the Sun. It will take 10,500 years to complete its orbit.

- In 2005 the Hubble Space Telescope spotted a KBO larger than Pluto, with its own moon. It has been named Eris. It was nicknamed the 'tenth planet'.

The most well-known Kuiper-Belt Object (KBO) is Pluto (see page 34). It was discovered in 1930, but the next Kuiper-Belt object was not discovered until 1992. More than a thousand have been found since. Many are as large as Pluto, and some have other objects orbiting around them.

The Oort Cloud

Much further out into space than the Kuiper Belt is a giant cloud of comets known as the Oort Cloud. The cloud, which is named after the Dutch astronomer, Jan Oort, is between 30,000 au to 100,000 au from the Sun. There may be a million billion comets here. The comets may have formed near the outer planets, and have been thrown into the far reaches of the Solar System by the gravity of the gas giants. We don't really know if the Oort Cloud exists since the objects in it are too distant and too small to be seen.

Sedna

In 2003, astronomers discovered an object like a small object more than 90 au (about 13 billion kilometres) from the Sun. They named it Sedna. It is about two-thirds the size of Pluto, and very red. It is the most distant object ever found in the Solar System. It is between the Kuiper Belt and the Oort cloud, leading astronomers to think that there is an inner Oort cloud, too.

Photographs of the trans-Neptunian object Eris, taken on successive days. Eris is between the two vertical markers.

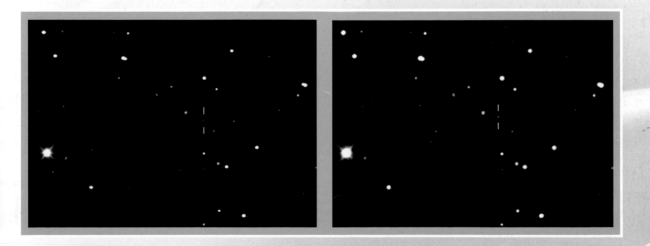

Pluto

Pluto is one of the icy bodies in the Kuiper Belt (see page 32). It was discovered in 1930, and for many decades it was considered to be a planet, along with the other eight. However, during the 1990s, many new bodies similar to Pluto were discovered in the Kuiper Belt, and many astronomers began to think that Pluto should not be classed as a planet after all.

A computer-enhanced photograph of Pluto, taken by the Hubble Space Telescope.

From planet to dwarf

After years of heated discussion, the decision to demote Pluto was taken by experts at the International Astronomical Union (IAU) in 2006. Pluto is now officially a 'dwarf planet', along with Ceres, a large object in the asteroid belt, and a Kuiper-Belt object called Eris (previously nicknamed Xena).

Orbit and spin

Pluto's orbit is very different to the planets' orbits. It is stretched in one direction, forming a shape called an ellipse (see page 6). The Sun is slightly to one side of the centre of the ellipse. This means that Pluto moves closer and further from the Sun as it orbits. At its closest, Pluto is 4,435 million kilometres from the Sun, and at its furthest it is 7,304 million kilometres away. It takes Pluto 248 Earth years to complete one orbit. For about 20 years of each orbit, Pluto is closer to the Sun than Neptune. Pluto's orbit is also tipped up slightly compared to the orbits of the planets.

SPACE DATA

Pluto

Diameter (equator):	2,390 km
Average distance from Sun:	5,870,000,000 km
Time to complete one orbit:	248 Earth years
Time to complete one spin:	6 Earth days 9 hours
Gravity at surface:	0.06 x Earth gravity
Surface temperature:	-225°C
Number of moons:	3

Pluto is also tipped quite far over on its side, and it spins in the opposite direction to all the planets. It also spins slowly, taking six Earth days and nine hours to complete a spin.

Pluto's structure

Astronomers have worked out what Pluto is probably like inside from knowing its mass and size. They think it has a large, rocky core, which is surrounded by a thick layer of water ice. The surface is probably covered with craters, and there may be polar ice caps of methane ice. When Pluto moves closer to the Sun, some ice turns to gas, making a thin atmosphere of nitrogen, methane and carbon monoxide.

The internal structure of Pluto. Astronomers don't know how large the core is.

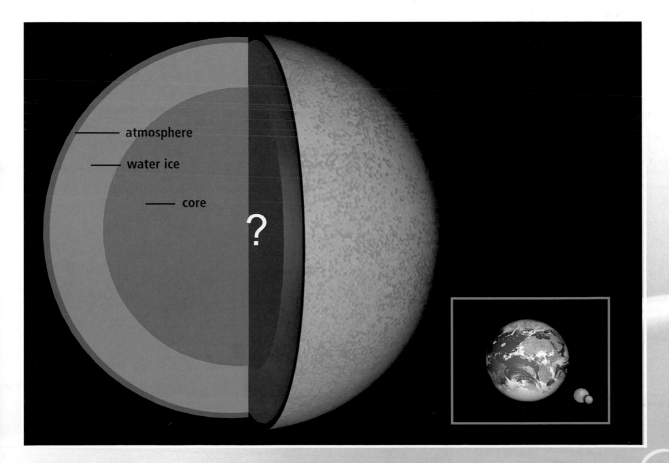

atmosphere

water ice

core

?

Pluto's Moons

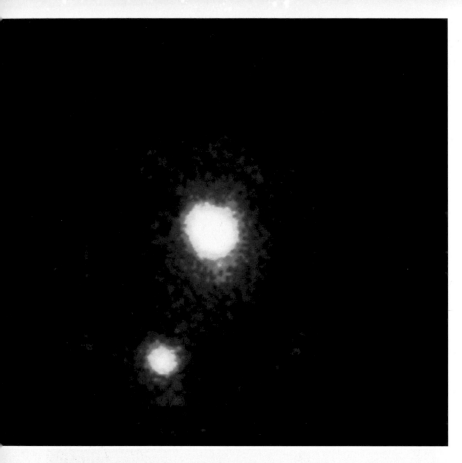

A photograph of Pluto (top) and Charon, taken by the Hubble Space Telescope.

Pluto has three moons, one large and two small. The large moon is called Charon. It is about half the width of Pluto (it is 1,186 kilometres across, compared to Pluto's 2,390 kilometres). No other moon in the Solar System is so large compared to its parent planet. The two small moons, named Nix and Hydra, are each somewhere between 50 and 150 kilometres across.

Orbiting each other

Charon's mass is about one eighth of Pluto's mass. It also orbits just 19,600 kilometres away from Pluto. Because of this, Charon and Pluto move around a spot in between them, a bit like a rod with weights on both ends. The spot is much closer to Pluto than Charon, but it is outside Pluto. So Pluto moves in a circle as Charon orbits around it. Because of this, Pluto and Charon can be thought of as a double dwarf planet.

How do we know?
Charon discovered

Although Pluto was found in 1930, Charon was not discovered until 1978. Astronomers at the US Naval Observatory were studying photographs of Pluto taken from Earth. The photographs showed Pluto just as a small disc, but they noticed a slight lump on one side. Further studies of other photographs showed that the lump was another object next to Pluto rather than a lump on Pluto itself. They had discovered Pluto's moon.

Pluto and Charon are also locked together in orbit. Pluto spins on its axis at the same rate as Charon orbits. And Charon spins on its axis at the same rate as Pluto. This means that the same side of Charon always faces Pluto, and the same side of Pluto always faces Charon. To an astronaut standing still on Pluto, Charon would always be in the same place in the sky. It also means that a day on Pluto is equal to a Charon month (a month is the time it takes for a moon to complete an orbit).

Charon's structure
Charon's structure is thought to be similar to Pluto's, with a rocky core covered in water ice. It probably has a cratered surface, too. Charon may have been formed when Pluto was broken up in a massive collision, or it may have been captured by Pluto's gravity as it drifted through space.

An artist's impression of Pluto (right) and Charon. Their surfaces may be cratered.

How we Observe the Outer Planets

Our knowledge of the outer planets and their moons has come from making careful observations. Astronomers observe the outer planets both from the Earth and through telescopes in space. We also send spacecraft called probes to the outer planets (see page 40).

Telescopes

An optical telescope makes distant objects appear larger. There are two main types of telescope. A refracting telescope uses a lens to collect and focus the light. A reflecting telescope uses a mirror instead. The larger the mirror or lens, the more light that can be collected, and the more detail that can be seen in an object. Most astronomers use reflecting telescopes because it is easier to build a large mirror than a large lens. Very large telescopes are needed to study objects in the outer Solar System because they are such an enormous distance away.

The protective dome of the William Herschel Telescope (WHT) *in the Canary Islands.*

Computer help

The image made by a telescope's lens or mirror is viewed with an eyepiece. More often, it is digitised in the same way as a digital camera records an image, so that it can be viewed and processed on a computer. This allows images to be enhanced to show up more detail. A computer can also automatically compare images taken at different times to detect objects moving against the background of stars. This is how new moons and Kuiper Belt Objects are discovered.

The **Hubble Space Telescope** *in orbit above the Earth.*

Getting a clear picture

Swirling air in the Earth's atmosphere makes light from space bend slightly before it reaches the ground, which is why stars twinkle at night. The latest, high-tech research telescopes use a computerised system called adaptive optics, which changes the shape of the mirror hundreds of times a second to cancel out the distortions caused by the atmosphere.

Space telescopes

Space telescopes, such as the Hubble Space Telescope, are telescopes that are up in space. They have two advantages over ground-based telescopes. First, the atmosphere does not distort their images. Secondly, they can detect types of rays that cannot get through the Earth's atmosphere, such as X-rays and ultraviolet rays, which can tell us more about the planets.

Space facts

Distance views

● Objects in the Kuiper Belt look very small from Earth. For example, Pluto looks about the same size as a pinhead a kilometre away.

● The Hubble Space Telescope is powerful enough to detect objects just a few kilometres across in the Kuiper Belt, more than five billion kilometres away.

How we Explore the Outer Planets

To find out more about the outer planets, we send robot spacecraft called probes to them. The probes take close-up photographs and gather other data about the planets and their moons.

Getting into orbit

Space is only a hundred kilometres away, but the Earth's strong gravity makes it very hard to get there. A spacecraft must reach 28,000 kilometres per hour to stay in orbit. Otherwise, gravity will pull it back to the Earth's surface. Reaching the other planets is much harder than getting into orbit. To travel to the outer planets, a probe must escape from the Earth's gravity completely. To do this, it must accelerate to 40,000 kilometres per hour.

A probe needs a huge push to lift it into orbit and to accelerate it fast enough to escape velocity. The push comes from extremely powerful launch vehicles, such as rockets and space shuttles. Their engines produce huge thrust, and they also work in space, where there is no air. Once a probe is travelling fast enough, it is released by its launch vehicle to continue its journey.

An Ariane 5 launch vehicle, carrying two satellites, waiting for lift-off.

Inside the Launch Control Centre for the Apollo 12 mission.

Space Facts

- *Voyager 2*'s journey to the outer planets was so carefully planned that it arrived just a minute late at Uranus, more than eight years after leaving Earth.

- The *Cassini-Huygens* probe to Saturn used the gravity of Earth, Venus and Jupiter to reach Saturn.

Plotting a path

It takes years to travel to the outer planets. Probes fly on a curved path (or trajectory) so that they meet a planet in its orbit. The path to the planet must be carefully planned, and the probe must be launched at a particular time so that it intercepts its target planet as the planet orbits.

Probes to the outer planets use the gravity of other planets to speed up and change direction to reach their destination. This manoeuvre is known as a gravity assist. Using gravity assists means that a probe does not need to carry lots of fuel for manoeuvring.

Anatomy of a probe

The main parts of a probe are its propulsion unit, a communications aerial, sensors that gather information, and a power source for its electronic circuits. The aerial detects radio signals from Earth that control the probe, and sends data signals back to Earth. Probes to the outer planets have nuclear power sources because they travel too far from the Sun to use solar arrays, panels of solar cells that turn sunlight into electricity.

The Future

What is left to find out about the outer planets, and how will we observe them and explore them in the future? And what does the future hold for the planets and moons themselves?

Future observations and probes

We really know very little about the outer planets. Observations of the planets and data sent back by probes have answered many questions that astronomers had in the past, but they also throw up new questions.

To find out more, we need to use more sophisticated telescopes ground-based telescopes and space telescopes that will see more detail. These telescopes will also allow us to discover more new Kuiper Belt Objects, and more moons around the outer planets. The replacement for the aging Hubble Space Telescope, the James Webb Space Telescope, will give much clearer views of the planets when it is launched in 2013.

Astronomers are keen to send new probes to the outer planets. For example, astronomers want to send a mission to Jupiter's moon Europa to search for signs of life in its oceans.

An artist's impression of the New Horizons *probe visiting the Kuiper Belt.*

Space Fact

Exploring the Kuiper Belt

● The *New Horizons* space probe has already left Earth, bound for Pluto. *New Horizons* was launched in early 2006, and will reach Pluto in 2015 to find out more about this icy world and its moons. Then it will set off to explore other objects in the Kuiper Belt.

New propulsion systems

Future probes to the outer planets may use new propulsion systems to make their journeys quicker. One idea is for a spacecraft to carry a solar sail. This is a very thin sail, perhaps 500 metres across. Radiation from the Sun would push on the sail, accelerating the craft to speeds up to 100 kilometres per second. Finding faster ways to get to the outer planets will be important if we plan to send astronauts in the future.

Important knowledge

You might ask why astronomers need to know about planets so far from Earth. One important reason is that these worlds can tell us a lot about the history of the Earth. For example, studies of Saturn's moon Titan could tell us what the Earth was like in its early years, and possibly even how life began here. And icy cold Kuiper Belt Objects may tell us about the materials that formed our Solar System in the first place.

An artist's impression of three solar-sail powered spacecraft cruising through the Solar System.

Timeline of Discovery

1610   Italian astronomer Galileo discovers Jupiter's four large moons using one of the very first optical telescopes.

1659   Dutch astronomer Christiaan Huygens describes Saturn's rings.

1781   The planet Uranus is discovered by German astronomer William Herschel.

1846   German astronomer Johann Galle discovers the planet Neptune. The position in space of Neptune was calculated by mathematicians.

1930   Pluto is discovered by American astronomer Clyde Tombaugh.

1972   *Pioneer 10*, the first probe to the outer planets, is launched.

1973   *Pioneer 10* makes a fly-by of Jupiter. It takes the first close-up photographs of the Solar System's largest planet.

1973   *Pioneer 11* is launched on its journey to Jupiter and Saturn.

1974   *Pioneer 11* flies past Jupiter.

1978   Pluto's moon Charon is discovered by astronomers at the US Naval Observatory.

One of the identical Pioneer probes that were the first to visit Jupiter.

1977   The probes *Voyager 1* and *Voyager 2* are launched.

1979   *Voyager 1* arrives at Jupiter. It sends back close-up images of the Great Red Spot, a giant storm system.

1979   *Voyager 2* arrives at Jupiter. It sends back pictures of volcanoes on Jupiter's moon, Io.

1979   *Pioneer 11* becomes the first probe to visit Saturn. It takes the first close-up photographs of Saturn's rings.

1980   *Voyager 1* arrives at Saturn.

1981   *Voyager 2* arrives at Saturn.

1986   *Voyager 2* becomes the first (and so far the only) probe to fly past Uranus. It discovers 10 new moons and the planet's magnetic field.

1989   *Voyager 2* becomes the first (and so far the only) probe to fly past Neptune. It discovers Neptune's rings.

1989   The *Galileo* probe is launched on its journey to Jupiter.

1992   The first Kuiper Belt Object is discovered.

1995   The *Galileo* probe releases a smaller probe that descends into Jupiter's atmosphere.

1997   The *Cassini-Huygens* probe is launched on its journey to Saturn.

2004   *Cassini-Huygens* enters orbit around Saturn.

2005   *Huygens* descends to the surface of Titan.

2005   Images from the Hubble Space Telescope reveal a large icy Kuiper Belt Object, which has been named Eris.

2006   The *New Horizons* probe lifts off for Pluto, Charon and the Kuiper Belt. It is due to arrive in 2015.

An astronaut servicing the Hubble Space Telescope *from a space shuttle in 1993.*

Glossary

ammonia A substance made up of nitrogen and hydrogen. It is normally a gas on Earth. Ammonia ice is the frozen form of ammonia.

asteroid A rocky object that orbits the Sun, but that is not large enough to be a planet. Most asteroids orbit between the orbits of Mars and Jupiter.

astronomer A scientist who studies planets, moons and other objects in space.

atmosphere A layer of gas that surrounds a planet or moon.

comet A small, icy object that orbits the Sun.

crater A dish-shaped hole in the surface of a planet or moon.

ellipse A squashed circle.

gravity A force that attracts all objects to each other.

ice cap A layer of ice at the pole of a planet.

jet stream A high speed wind that blows around the Earth in the upper layers of the atmosphere.

Kuiper Belt A region of space beyond Neptune where there are thousands of icy bodies orbiting the Earth.

Kuiper Belt Object (KBO) Any object that is part of the Kuiper Belt.

lava The name for molten rock after it comes out of a volcano.

magnetic field The region around a magnet where its effects can be felt.

moon An object that orbits a planet, but that is not part of a planet's rings.

nebula A giant cloud of gas and dust in space.

nuclear reaction When the nucleus of an atom splits apart, or loses or gains some particles.

orbit 1) Moving around the Sun or a planet; 2) The path that an object takes as it moves around the Sun or a planet.

planet An object in space that orbits around the Sun, but that is not part of a large group of objects, such as asteroids or comets.

pole The point on the surface of a planet in line with the planet's axis.

pressure A push made by a gas or a liquid on anything that is in the gas or liquid.

probe A spacecraft sent into space to send back information about the Sun, other planets or moons.

radiation Energy that moves from place to place in the form of waves or particles, such as X-rays and infra-red rays.

shepherd moon A moon whose gravity shapes a planet's rings by attracting the particles in the ring.

solar array A panel of solar cells that turn sunlight into electricity.

water ice Water in its solid form.

water vapour The gas form of water.

Further Information

Books

11 Planets: A New View of the Solar System
David A. Aguilar
National Geographic Children's Books, 2008

The Outer Planets (The Universe)
Tim Goss and Geza Gyuk
Heinemann, 2007

When is a Planet Not a Planet?
Elaine Scott
Clarion, 2007

Organizations

National Aeronautics & Space
Administration (NASA)
Organization that runs the US space
program
www.nasa.gov

International Astronomical Union (IAU)
The official world astronomy organization,
responsible for naming stars, planets,
moons and other objects in space
www.iau.org

Jet Propulsion Laboratory (JPL)
Centre responsible for NASA's robot space
probes
www.jpl.nasa.gov

European Space Agency (ESA)
Organization responsible for space flight
and exploration of European countries
www.esa.int

The Planetary Society
Organization devoted to the exploration of
the Solar System
www.planetary.org

Websites

http://nssdc.gsfc.nasa.gov/planetary/
factsheet/
All the facts and figures you could ever
need about the outer planets

www.nineplanets.org
Lots of information about the planets

http://sse.jpl.nasa.gov/kids/index.cfm
NASA pages for children about exploring
the Solar System

http://hubblesite.org/
NASA's home page for the Hubble Space
Telescope. Fantastic images of the outer
planets in the gallery

http://saturn.jpl.nasa.gov/home/index.cfm
Home page of the Cassini-Huygens probe
to Saturn and Titan

http://www.jwst.nasa.gov/
Home page of the James Webb Space
Telescope

http://www.keckobservatory.org/
All about the Keck telescopes in Hawaii

Index

Numbers in **bold** indicate pictures.